Python B

The Crash Course for Understanding the Basics of Python Computer Language

More Free and Bargain Books at

KindleBookSpot.com

Table Of Contents

Introduction

I want to thank you and congratulate you for downloading the book, "Python Programming for Beginners."

This book contains proven steps and strategies on how to master the basic elements of the Python programming language.

This eBook will teach you important information regarding Python. It will explain concepts and ideas that are being used by Python programmers. Additionally, it will give you actual codes and statements. That means you'll know the theoretical and practical aspects of the Python language.

In this book you will learn:

- What Python is
- How to use Python
- Common Python data
- And much more!

Thanks again for downloading this book. I hope you enjoy it!

Chapter 1: What is Python?

Python is an advanced and structured programming language. You can use it to accomplish various programming tasks. Additionally, Python is an open-source language: thousands of computer experts across the globe are using and improving it on a daily basis. A Dutch programmer named Guido Van Rossum created Python in the early part of the 90s. He named it after a comedy show titled Monty Python's Flying Circus.

Computer experts consider Python as a powerful programming language. System administrators are using it to develop different types of computer software. Actually, Python has greatly helped in improving Linux systems. Most of Linux's main components are written using Python. IT professors also use this language to teach basic programming. That means Python is versatile, powerful, and easy to learn.

Before execution, this programming language gets compiled into bytecode automatically. The system saves the bytecode onto the hard disk. That means the user doesn't have to perform compilation unless changes are made on the source. Additionally, Python is a dynamically typed programming language that allows (but doesn't require) object-oriented constructs and features.

Unlike other programming languages, Python considers whitespace as an important part of its codes. In fact, the whitespace's significance is the most distinctive attribute of Python. Rather than block delimiters (which is being used by C programming languages), Python uses indentation to indicate the starting point and endpoint of code blocks.

Another cool aspect of Python is that it is available for ALL platforms. You can easily install and use Python on Linux, Macintosh, and Windows computers. That means computer programs written using this language are extremely portable: you can use them with any available platform.

Chapter 2: Python's Interactive Mode

The Python programming language has 2 different modes:

1. Normal – In this mode, you'll run the scripted and completed Python files using the built-in interpreter.

2. Interactive – This is a command line program that can give instant feedback for each of your statements. This mode gives feedback while performing previous statements stored in the machine's memory. Technically, the interactive mode evaluates statements individually and holistically while new ones are being entered into the Python interpreter.

This chapter will focus on the interactive mode. To activate it, just enter "python" without adding any argument. This is an excellent way of learning the programming language: you'll play around statements and syntax variations. After typing "python," the screen will show you a message similar to the one below:

```
$ python
Python 3.0b3 (r30b3:66303, Sep  5 2008, 14:01:02) [MSC v.1500 32 bit (Intel)]
on win32
Type "help", "copyright", "credits" or "license" for more information.
>>>
```

Important Note: If Python doesn't work, make sure that you have set your path properly.

Notice that the message has ">>>" at the end. These symbols indicate that you are using Python's interactive mode. Here, the system will immediately run whatever you type. Actually, if you'll type 1 + 1, Python will give you 2. You can use this mode to become familiar with Python and test its capabilities. If you have learned new statements, activate the interactive mode and check them one by one.

The image below shows an interactive session:

```
>>> 5
5
>>> print (5*7)
35
>>> "hello" * 4
'hellohellohellohello'
>>> "hello".__class__
<type 'str'>
```

As you can see, Python's interactive environment is an excellent learning and programming tool. However, you have to be extremely careful when using it since it can be confusing sometimes. For instance, the image below shows a Python script that is considered valid in the interactive mode:

```
if 1:
   print("True")
print("Done")
```

If you'll use this script as shown in the interactive mode, you'll get a surprising result:

```
>>> if 1:
...     print("True")
...     print("Done")
  File "<stdin>", line 3
    print("Done")
SyntaxError: invalid syntax
```

The Python interpreter says that the second print's indentation is unexpected. Before writing the next statement, you need to end the first one (i.e. the "if" statement) using a blank line. For instance, you must enter the statements using this format:

```
if 1:
    print("True")
        Blank Line
print("Done")
```

This will give the following result:

```
>>> if 1:
...     print("True")
...
True
      print("Done")
Done
>>>
```

The Interactive Mode

You may use "-i" to activate the interactive mode. This flag will stop Python from closing when the program is done. Computer programmers use this flag a lot, especially during the prototyping and debugging stages. Here's an example:

```
python -i hello.py
```

Chapter 3: The Basics

In this section, you'll learn about the basics of the Python programming language. The following pages will teach you how to create programs using Python. Additionally, you'll know about the different parts of Python statements such as strings and variables. Study this chapter carefully because it can help you become a great Python user.

How to Create Python Programs

In general, programs created using Python are just ordinary text files. That means you can edit them with typical text editors. Use your favorite editor: you can create or improve Python programs using any text editing software. However, it would be great if you can use one that has syntax highlighting for Python statements.

Your First Program

Inexperienced programmers start their Python journey by writing the "Hello, World!" program. Here, the program simply states "Hello, World!" and then closes itself. Try this simple exercise:

1. Access your favorite text editor.

2. Create a file and save it as "hello.py." Inside that file, enter the following line:

```python
print('Hello, world!')
```

The "Hello, World!" program utilizes PRINT, a function that sends the parameters of a statement to the machine's terminal. The PRINT function adds a newline character to the statement's output. Thus, it automatically transfers the cursor to the subsequent line.

Important Note: For Python version 2, PRINT is considered as a statement instead of a function. That means you may use it without any parenthesis. In this situation, PRINT does two things:

- *It sends the whole line to the terminal*

- *It allows users to indicate multiline statements by placing a comma after the last character.*

You've just completed your own program. Now, you are ready to run it using Python. Notice that this procedure differs based on the OS (i.e. operating system) you are using.

For Windows computers:

1. Create a new folder. You should only use this folder for Python computer programs. Save the hello.py file in this folder. For this exercise, let's assume that you named the folder: "C:\pythonfiles"

2. Access the Start menu and choose "Run..."

3. Open the OS' terminal by typing "cmd" in the dialogue box.

4. Type cd \pythonfiles and hit Enter. This action will set the pythonfiles folder as the directory.

5. Run the program by typing hello.py (i.e. the program's filename).

For Mac computers:

- Create a folder that will be used for Python programs only. For this exercise, name this folder "pythonfiles" and save it in your computer's Home folder (i.e. the one that holds folders for Music, Movies, Pictures, Documents, etc.).

- Save the hello.py program into the pythonfiles folder.

- Access the Applications section of your computer, go to Utilities, and activate the Terminal software.

- Enter <u>cd pythonfiles</u> into the dialogue box and press Enter.

- Run the Hello, World! program by typing "<u>python ./hello.py</u>."

For Linux computers:

- Create a folder and name it "pythonfiles." Then, save the hello.py file in it.

- Activate the computer's terminal program. Follow these instructions:

  - For KDE users – go to the main menu and choose "Run Command..."

  - For GNOME users – go to the main menu, access the Applications section, open Accessories, and choose Terminal.

- Enter "<u>cd ~/pythonpractice</u>."

- Run the program by typing "<u>python. hello.py</u>."

<u>*The Outcome*</u>

The screen must show:

Hello, World!

That's it. If your computer screen shows this message, you did an excellent job. You're one step closer to being a great Python programmer.

The Variables and Strings in the Python Language

This section will focus on strings and variables. As a beginner, you should know that these two types of data play a huge role in the Python programming language.

The Variables

Basically, variables are things that hold changeable values. That means you can consider variables as boxes that can hold different kinds of stuff. Keep in mind that you can use variables to keep different things. For now, however, let's use them for storing numbers. Check the screenshot below:

```
lucky = 7
print (lucky)
7
```

The code above generates a variable named "lucky." Afterward, it assigns the variable to a number (i.e. 7). If you'll "ask" Python about the data stored in lucky, you'll get 7 as the response.

You may also edit the value inside variables. For instance:

```
changing = 3
print (changing)
3

changing = 9
print (changing)
9

different = 12
print (different)
12
print (changing)
9

changing = 15
print (changing)
15
```

With the codes above, you saved a variable named "changing," assigned the number 3 to it, and confirmed that the first statement is correct. Afterward, you assigned the number 9 to the variable, and asked the system about the new content. The Python language replaced 3 with 9.

Then, you created a new variable named "different." You assigned the number 12 for this variable. That means you currently have two different variables, namely: changing and different. These variables hold different data – setting another value for one of them won't affect the other.

Python allows you to assign the value of an existing variable to a different one. For instance:

```
red = 5
blue = 10
print (red, blue)
5 10

yellow = red
print (yellow, red, blue)
5 5 10

red = blue
print (yellow, red, blue)
5 10 10
```

To prevent confusion, remember that the variable's name is always shown on the left side of the assignment operator (i.e. the "=" sign). The variable's value, on the other hand, is displayed on the operator's right side. That means for each variable, you'll see the name first followed by the value.

At first, the code created two variables: red and blue. Then it assigned different values for each: 5 and 10, respectively. Notice that you can place different arguments on the PRINT function to make it show several items in a single line. As the result shows, red holds 5 while blue stores 10.

Then, the code created another variable and named it "yellow." Afterward, the code instructed Python that yellow's value should be identical to that of red. Because of that, Python assigned the number 5 to yellow.

Next, the code instructed Python that red's value must be changed so that it is equal to that of blue. The value of blue is 10 so Python assigns that number to red (the number 5 is "thrown away"). At the last part of the screenshot, Python indicates the value of red, blue and yellow: 10, 10, 5, respectively.

Wait! The code told Python that the value of yellow must be equal to that of red, didn't it? Why does the screenshot show that yellow's value is 5 even though red's is 10? It's simple. The code instructed the Python language that yellow should have red's value at the moment it was coded. The connection between red and yellow stopped as soon as Python assigned a value to the latter. Yellow received 5 - and 5 will stay regardless of what happens to its original source (unless a new statement is given).

The Strings

Basically, strings are lists of characters that follow a certain arrangement.

What is a "character?" Let's relate this concept with a physical object: the keyboard. Anything you can enter using a keyboard is considered as a character (e.g. numbers, letters, punctuation marks, etc.).

For instance, "Birthday" and "Halloween" are strings. These strings are formed by letters (i.e. characters). You can also add spaces in your strings: "good morning" contains 12 characters: good = 4, space = 1, morning = 7. Currently, you can include any number of characters in your Python strings. That means there are no limits when it comes to the quantity of characters that you can use. Actually, you can even create a string that has no character in it (programmers call it an "empty string.").

With Python, you can declare strings in three different ways:

1. (') – Using single quotation marks

2. (") – Using double quotation marks

3. (""") – Using triple quotation marks

You can use any of these methods. However, make sure that you will be consistent regarding your string declarations. Begin and end your strings using the same declaration. Check the screenshot below:

```
>>> print ('I am a single quoted string')
I am a single quoted string
>>> print ("I am a double quoted string")
I am a double quoted string
>>> print ("""I am a triple quoted string""")
I am a triple quoted string
```

As you can see, quotation marks start and end strings. By default, Python will consider the quotation marks in your statements as markers for the beginning or end of strings.

In some situations, however, you have to include quotation marks in your statements. That means you must stop Python from ending your statements prematurely (i.e. when it sees the quotation marks in your codes). You can accomplish this using a backslash. By adding a backslash right before the quotation marks, you're telling Python that those marks are included in the string. The act of putting a backslash before a different symbol is known as "escaping" that particular symbol.

Important Note: When adding a backslash to your Python strings, you still need to "escape" it (i.e. place a backslash before the needed backslash). This action will inform Python that the backslash must be used as an ordinary symbol. Analyze the screenshot below:

```
>>> print ("So I said, \"You don't know me! You'll never understand me!\"")
So I said, "You don't know me! You'll never understand me!"
>>> print ('So I said, "You don\'t know me! You\'ll never understand me!"')
So I said, "You don't know me! You'll never understand me!"
>>> print ("This will result in only three backslashes: \\ \\ \\")
This will result in only three backslashes: \ \ \
>>> print ("""The double quotation mark (\") is used to indicate direct quotations.""")
The double quotation mark (") is used to indicate direct quotations.
```

After analyzing the examples above, you'll realize that only the characters used to quote strings must be escaped. This simple rule makes Python statements easy to read.

To help you understand strings further, let's visit your first Python program:

```
>>> print("Hello, world!")
Hello, world!
```

Well, it seems you have used strings even before you learned about them. You may also concatenate strings in the Python programming language. Concatenation is the process of combining two different strings by adding a "+"

sign between them. Let's use the same program again:

```
>>> print ("Hello, " + "world!")
Hello, world!
```

In the example above, "Hello," and "world!" are entered as separate strings. This is done by enclosing both strings in quotation marks. Then, the "+" sign is added between the strings to combine (i.e. concatenate) them. Did you see the space between the comma and the quotation mark? That space is mandatory: without it, you'll get the following string:

```
Hello,world!
```

Python also allows you to repeat strings. That means you won't have to type the same thing several times. To repeat strings, just use the asterisk:

```
>>> print ("bouncy, " * 10)
bouncy, bouncy, bouncy, bouncy, bouncy, bouncy, bouncy, bouncy, bouncy, bouncy,
```

Lastly, you can utilize "len()" to count the characters that form any string. You just have to place the string you want to check inside the parentheses. Here's an example:

```
>>> print (len("Hello, world!"))
13
```

Variables and Strings – How to Use Them Together

Now that you know how strings and variables work, you're ready to use them together.

As discussed earlier, variables can hold different types of information – even strings. Here's an example:

```
question = "What did you have for lunch?"
print (question)
```

The program above creates a variable named "question." Then, it stores the string "What did you have for lunch?" inside that variable. Lastly, it instructs Python to give out the string.

It is important to note that you should not enclose the variable with quotation marks. By omitting quotation marks, you are telling Python that you are using "question" as a variable, not as a string. If you'll enclose the variable using quotation marks, Python will consider it as an ordinary string. It will give out "question" rather than "What did you have for lunch?"

How to Combine Strings and Numbers

Analyze the screenshot below:

```python
print ("Please give me a number: ")
number = raw_input()

plusTen = number + 10
print ("If we add 10 to your number, we get " + plusTen)
```

This code is designed to accept a number from the programmer, add ten to that number, and give out the sum. If you'll run it, however, you'll get the following error message:

```
Traceback (most recent call last):
  File "test.py", line 7, in <module>
    print "If we add 10 to your number, we get " + plusTen
TypeError: cannot concatenate 'str' and 'int' objects
```

What's happening here? Instead of giving out a number, Python shows "TypeError." This message means there is an issue with the information entered. To be specific, Python cannot determine how to combine the two kinds of data being used: strings and integers.

For instance, Python assumes that "number" (i.e. a variable) contains a string, rather than a number. If the programmer types in "15," Python will think that the variable holds a 2-character string: 1 and 5. What can you do to inform Python that 15 is a number?

Additionally, when asking for the answer, you are instructing Python to combine a number (i.e. plusTen) and a string. The programming language doesn't know how to accomplish that. Python can only combine two strings. How can you make Python treat numbers as strings, so you can use it with a different string?

Fortunately, you have two powerful functions at your disposal:

1. str() – This function can convert numbers into strings.

2. int() – This function can convert strings into numbers.

When using these functions, you just have to place the string/number you want to convert inside the parentheses. If you will apply this method to the code given earlier, you will get the following result:

```
print ("Please give me a number:",)
response = raw_input()

number = int(response)
plusTen = number + 10

print ("If we add 10 to your number, we get " + str(plusTen))
```

The Fundamental Concepts

Python has 5 basic concepts, namely:

1. Scope – For large systems, you have to limit the relationship between codes. This is important if you want to prevent errors or unpredictable system behaviors. If you won't restrict the effect of your codes on other codes, the entire system might get confused.

   You can control the "scope" of your codes by assigning specific name groups to each programmer. For instance, one programmer will use the names of countries while another one uses names of animals. This technique can help in limiting the connections between your Python codes.

2. Objects – Similar to other object-oriented languages, Python uses code and data groups.

   In Python, you'll create (i.e. instantiate) objects using "Classes" (a set of templates used in this programming language). Objects possess "attributes," which store the different pieces of data and code that form the object.

   Accessing an object's attribute is easy:

   i. Enter the object's name and place a dot after it.
   ii. Specify the name of the attribute/s you want to access.

3. Namespaces – Python has dir(), a preinstalled function that can help you understand namespaces. After starting Python's interpreter, you can use dir() to show the objects in the default or current namespace. Check the screenshot below:

```
Python 2.3.4 (#53, Oct 18 2004, 20:35:07) [MSC v.1200 32 bit (Intel)] on win32
Type "help", "copyright", "credits" or "license" for more information.
>>> dir()
['__builtins__', '__doc__', '__name__']
```

You can also use dir() to list the available names inside module namespaces. For this example, let's use type() on _builtins_ (an object from the screenshot above). This function, i.e. type(), allows us to know the file type of an object. See the screenshot below:

```
>>> type(__builtins__)
<type 'module'>
```

The image shows that _builtins_ is a module. That means you can use dir() to list the names inside _builtins_. You'll get this result:

```
>>> dir(__builtins__)
['ArithmeticError', ... 'copyright', 'credits', ... 'help', ... 'license', ... 'zip']
>>>
```

This concept is easy to understand. Basically, namespaces are places in which names can reside. Every name inside a namespace is completely different from those outside a namespace. Computer programmers refer to this "namespace layering" as "scope." In general, you should place names inside a namespace if those names have values. For instance:

```
>>> dir()
['__builtins__', '__doc__', '__name__']
>>> name = "Bob"
>>> import math
>>> dir()
['__builtins__', '__doc__', '__name__', 'math', 'name']
```

The image above shows that you can add names to any namespace just by using a simple statement (i.e. "import"). That code used the import statement to add "math" to the active namespace. If you want to know what that object is, you can run this command:

```
>>> math
<module 'math' (built-in)>
```

It says that "math" is a module. Thus, it has its own namespace. You can show the names inside math's namespace using the dir() function:

```
>>> dir(math)
['__doc__', '__name__', 'acos', 'asin', 'atan', 'atan2', 'ceil', 'cos', 'cosh', 'degrees', 'e',
'exp', 'fabs', 'floor', 'fmod', 'frexp', 'hypot', 'ldexp', 'log', 'log10', 'modf', 'pi', 'pow',
'radians', 'sin', 'sinh', 'sqrt', 'tan', 'tanh']
>>>
```

4. Case Sensitivity – Variables are always case-sensitive. That means "SMITH," "Smith," and "smith" are three different variables.

5. Tabs and Spaces Don't Mix – Since whitespaces are important in Python, keep in mind that tabs and spaces cannot be mixed. Be consistent while indenting your python statements. If you'll use spaces for indention, stick to that character. This is an important concept that many beginners forget about.

   Although tabs and spaces have the same appearance, they give different meanings when read by the Python interpreter. That means you'll experience errors or weird results if you'll mix them in your statements.

   Important Note: If you prefer to use spaces, make sure that you will hit the spacebar four times for each indention.

Chapter 4: Sequences

Sequences, one of the basic structures in programming, allow you to save values easily and efficiently. Python supports three types of sequences, namely: lists, tuples, and strings. Let's discuss each sequence in detail:

Lists

As their name suggests, lists are collections of values that follow a certain arrangement. You can use square brackets to create a list. For instance, you can use the statement below to initialize an empty list:

```
spam = []
```

You should use commas to separate values. Here's a sample list:

```
spam = ["bacon", "eggs", 42]
```

You can place different kinds of values inside the same list. For instance, the list above holds numbers and letters.

Similar to characters within a string, you can access listed items using indices that start at zero. Accessing a listed item is easy. You just have to specify the name of the list where that item belongs. Then, indicate the number of the item inside the list. Enclose the number using square brackets. Here's an example:

```
>>> spam
['bacon', 'eggs', 42]
>>> spam[0]
'bacon'
>>> spam[1]
'eggs'
>>> spam[2]
42
```

Python also allows you to enter negative integers. These numbers are counted backwards, starting from the last item in the list.

```
>>> spam[-1]
42
>>> spam[-2]
'eggs'
>>> spam[-3]
'bacon'
```

You may use len() to determine the quantity of items inside a list. Check the image below:

```
>>> len(spam)
3
```

Lists are similar to typical variables in one aspect: they allow you to change the items inside them. Analyze the following example:

```
>>> spam = ["bacon", "eggs", 42]
>>> spam
['bacon', 'eggs', 42]
>>> spam[1]
'eggs'
>>> spam[1] = "ketchup"
>>> spam
['bacon', 'ketchup', 42]
```

ou can also slice strings:

```
>>> spam[1:]
['eggs', 42]
>>> spam[:-1]
['bacon', 'eggs']
```

Python offers different methods of adding items to any list. However, the easiest method is this:

```
>>> spam.append(10)
>>> spam
['bacon', 'eggs', 42, 10]
```

To remove items, you can apply the "del" statement onto the list. Here's an example:

```
>>> spam
['bacon', 'and', 'eggs', 42, 10]
>>> del spam[1]
>>> spam
['bacon', 'eggs', 42, 10]
>>> spam[0]
'bacon'
>>> spam[1]
'eggs'
>>> spam[2]
42
>>> spam[3]
10
```

Lists automatically "fix" themselves after each item deletion. That means you won't see any gap in the numbering of items.

Tuples

Tuples and lists are similar except for one thing: tuples cannot be edited. After creating a tuple, you won't be able to change it in any way. You can't expand, edit, or delete the elements within a tuple. If you'll ignore this immutability, you can say that lists and tuples are identical.

You should use commas when declaring tuples:

```
unchanging = "rocks", 0, "the universe"
```

Sometimes, you have to differentiate tuples using parentheses. This process is similar to performing several assignments using the same line. Here's a simple example:

```
foo, bar = "rocks", 0, "the universe" # 3 elements here
foo, bar = "rocks", (0, "the universe") # 2 elements here because the second element is a tuple
```

Strings

You've already learned about strings. However, it is important to discuss it again as a Python sequence. For other programming languages, you can access the characters elements inside strings using square brackets (known as the subscript operator). This method is also effective in Python:

```
>>> "Hello, world!"[0]
'H'
>>> "Hello, world!"[1]
'e'
>>> "Hello, world!"[2]
'l'
>>> "Hello, world!"[3]
'l'
>>> "Hello, world!"[4]
'o'
```

Python assigns numbers to indices using this formula: 0 – n1 (n represents the number of characters in the string). Check the screenshot below:

```
H  e  l  l  o  ,  _  w  o  r  l  d  !
0  1  2  3  4  5  6  7  8  9  10 11 12
```

Indices work with the characters that come right after them. For negative indices, you should count backwards:

```
>>> "Hello, world!"[-2]
'd'
>>> "Hello, world!"[-9]
'o'
>>> "Hello, world!"[-13]
'H'
>>> "Hello, world!"[-1]
'!'
```

35

Unlike other programming languages, Python allows you to place up to 2 numbers inside square brackets. You can do this using a colon (i.e. ":"). For sequences that concentrate on numeric indices, the combination of brackets and colons returns the portion between the indices. This technique is called "slicing." If you'll slice a string, you will get "substrings." Analyze the screenshot below:

```
>>> "Hello, world!"[3:9]
'lo, wo'
>>> string = "Hello, world!"
>>> string[:5]
'Hello'
>>> string[-6:-1]
'world'
>>> string[-9:]
'o, world!'
>>> string[:-8]
'Hello'
>>> string[:]
'Hello, world!'
```

The statements given above show an important rule:

"If you'll omit a number, Python assumes the missing number as the start or end of that particular sequence (depending on the position of the missing number)."

Dictionaries

Dictionaries are similar to lists. Unlike tuples, dictionaries allow users to modify their content. That means you may add, edit, and delete the elements of any dictionary. The main difference between lists and dictionaries is this: dictionaries don't bind their elements to any number.

A dictionary's element has two aspects: (1) the key and (2) the value. If you'll call the key of a dictionary, you'll get the values related to that particular key. Computer programmers consider lists as special dictionaries, where numbers represent the key of each element.

How to Use a Dictionary

You should use curly braces when declaring a dictionary. Also, you should use the following format when declaring elements for a dictionary: (1) enter the key of the element, (2) add a colon, and (3) assign the value. Here's an example:

```
>>> definitions = {"guava": "a tropical fruit", "python": "a programming language", "the answer": 42}
>>> definitions
{'python': 'a programming language', 'the answer': 42, 'guava': 'a tropical fruit'}
>>> definitions["the answer"]
42
>>> definitions["guava"]
'a tropical fruit'
>>> len(definitions)
3
```

Additionally, adding elements to dictionaries is simple and easy. It's like adding an ordinary variable:

```
>>> definitions["new key"] = "new value"
>>> definitions
{'python': 'a programming language', 'the answer': 42, 'guava': 'a tropical fruit', 'new key': 'new value'}
```

Chapter 5: The Different Types of Data

Basically, data types define an object's capabilities. In other languages, the effectiveness of an operation is tested by ensuring that the object cannot be stored where the operation is going to be performed. This system is known as static typing.

However, Python uses a different approach. This programming language allows you to store the object's data type inside that object. Python also checks the validity of each operation as soon as you run them. Programmers refer to this system as dynamic typing.

This chapter focuses on the different kinds of data that you can use with Python.

The Standard Types

Python has a set of standard data types. These types are pre-installed into this programming language. Let's divide these types into small groups. This section will use the hierarchy system used in Python's official documentation:

The Numeric Types

- int – This stands for integers. For Python 2.x, "int" is identical to C longs.

- long – It stands for long integers whose length is non-limited. You'll find this type in systems that use Python 2.x.

- float – This stands for floating-point numbers. Float is the equivalent of doubles in C.

- complex – This type is composed of complex numbers.

The Sequences

- list

- tuple

- byte – This is a sequence of numbers within the 0-255 range. You'll find bytes in systems that use Python 3.x.

- byte array – This is the mutable version of bytes.

- str – This stands for "String." Python 2.x systems represent strings as sequences of 8-bit items. Python 3.x systems, however, represent them as sequences of Unicode items.

The Sets

- set – This is an unorganized group of distinct objects.

- frozen set – This type is the immutable version of sets.

The Mappings

- dict – This stands for Python dictionaries. Computer programmers refer to this type as a "hashmap" or "associative array." In general, each element of a dictionary has a corresponding definition.

Mutable and Immutable Objects

In the Python language, data types are categorized based on the mutability of their contents. Keep in mind that immutable data types prevent you from changing the objects inside them. That means you'll succeed in slicing or reassigning the objects of mutable data.

Immutable ones, however, will give you an error message.

Here's an important principle that you should remember: variables are simple references to the objects inside a machine's memory. Let's assume that you paired an object and a variable using the following statement:

```
a = 1
s = 'abc'
l = ['a string', 456, ('a', 'tuple', 'inside', 'a', 'list')]
```

With the statement given above, you are making variables (i.e. 1, a, and s) point to certain objects. Python stores this relationship between variables and objects in the machine's memory. Thus, you can conveniently access objects whenever you want.

For the next example, let's say you performed a reassignment using the code below:

```
a = 7
s = 'xyz'
l = ['a simpler list', 99, 10]
```

In this new statement, you linked the variables to other objects. As you've learned earlier, you can only change mutable objects (1 [0] = 1 is good, but s [0] = "a" will give you an error message).

How to Create Objects of a Defined Type

- *Literal Integers* – You can enter literal integers in three different ways:

  - For decimal numbers – You can enter these numbers directly.

  - For hexadecimal numbers – You have to prepend oX or ox to enter this kind of number.

  - For octal literals – The method of entering these integers depends on the Python version you are using:

    - For Python 2.x – You must prepend a zero to enter octals.

    - For Python 3.x – You should prepend oO or oo to enter octals.

- *Floating Point Integers* – You can enter these numbers directly.

- *Long Integers* – You can enter a long integer in two ways:

  - Directly (112233445566778899 is considered as a long integer)

  - By appending the letter "L" (1L is considered as a long integer).

If a computation that involves short integers overflows, it is automatically converted into a long integer.

- *Complex Numbers* – You can enter this object by adding two numbers (i.e. a real number and an imaginary number). Then, enter these numbers by appending the letter "j." That means 11+2j and 11j are complex numbers.

- *Strings* – You can enter strings as single- or triple-quoted objects. The difference between these two types lies in their delimiters and their potential length. Single-quoted strings are restricted to one line only. You can enter single-quoted strings using pairs of single quotation or double quotation marks. Check the following example:

```
'foo' works, and
"moo" works as well,
     but
'bar" does not work, and
"baz' does not work either.
"quux'' is right out.
```

Triple-quoted strings are similar to their single-quoted counterparts, but they can cover multiple lines. Obviously, their delimiters (i.e. the quotation marks) should be matched. You must enter these strings using 3 single or double quotation marks. Here's an instructive screenshot for you:

```
'''foo''' works, and
"""moo""" works as well,
     but
'"'bar'"' does not work, and
"""baz''' does not work either.
'"'quux"'" is right out.
```

- *Tuples* - You can enter tuples using parentheses. Place commas between objects to separate them.

```
(10, 'Mary had a little lamb')
```

You can enter a single-element tuple by enclosing it in parentheses and adding a comma. Here's an example:

```
('this is a stupid tuple',)
```

- *Lists* - Lists work like tuples, though they require square brackets:

```
['abc', 1,2,3]
```

- *Dictionaries* – You can create "Python dicts" by listing some pairs of values and separating each pair using a colon. Use commas to separate dictionary entries. Then, enclose the statements using curly braces. Check the image below:

```
{ 'hello': 'world', 'weight': 'African or European?' }
```

Null Objects

Python uses "None" as a null pointer analogue. In this aspect, Python is similar to many programming languages. Actually, "None" isn't a null reference or a null pointer in itself – it is an object that only has one instance. You can use "None" as a default argument value for functions. In Python, you must compare objects against "None" using "is" instead of "==."

Chapter 6: The Errors That You Will Encounter

Python users encounter three kinds of errors: exceptions, logic errors, and syntax errors.

Exceptions

These errors occur when the Python interpreter cannot perform an action, though it knows what should be done. A good example would be running a Google search while you are offline: the machine knows what to do but it cannot accomplish it.

Logic Errors

Logic errors are extremely hard to find. Also, they are the most common errors that you'll get. Python programs that are affected by logic errors can still run. However, they may crash or produce unexpected results.

You can use a debugger to find and solve logic errors in your programs.

Syntax Errors

This is perhaps the most basic kind of error. A syntax error occurs when the Python interpreter cannot understand a code. According to programmers, syntax errors are fatal most of the time – you cannot execute codes that contain this error.

Syntax errors are often caused by typos, wrong arguments, or wrong indentation. That means you should inspect your codes for these mistakes whenever you encounter a syntax error.

Conclusion

Thank you again for downloading this book!

I hope this book was able to help you master the basics of Python.

The next step is to create your own programs using this powerful computer language.

Finally, if you enjoyed this book, then I'd like to ask you for a favor, would you be kind enough to leave a review for this book on Amazon? It'd be greatly appreciated!

Please leave a review on Amazon!

Thank you and good luck!

Bonus Book

SQL Bootcamp

Learn the Basics of SQL
Programming in 2 Weeks

More Free and Bargain Books at
KindleBookSpot.com

Table Of Contents

Introduction

I want to thank you and congratulate you for downloading the book, *"Learn the Basics of SQL Programming in 2 Weeks."*

This book contains proven steps and strategies on how to study the SQL programming language quickly and effectively.

This eBook will teach you the basics of SQL, a powerful computer language used in relational databases. Since this is a short book, it focuses on the most important aspects of SQL. It explains the basics of the language, the characteristics of database systems, the commands that you can use, and the constraints that you may apply on your databases. Basically, everything that you'll read in this book is designed to help you learn SQL in two weeks. This book doesn't have any irrelevant piece of information.

If you want to become a proficient SQL user, this is the book you need. Read this material carefully and analyze the syntaxes it contains. That way, you'll surely master the foundations of the SQL computer language.

Thanks again for downloading this book, I hope you enjoy it!

Chapter 1: SQL – Basic Information

This book offers a unique teaching approach: it will help you learn the fundamentals of the SQL programming language in 2 weeks. Additionally, it will provide you with examples that can aid you in mastering this language immediately.

Basically, SQL is a computer language used in databases. It involves data rows, column modifications, and database generation.

SQL - Structured Query Language

SQL is a language that you can use to store, manipulate, and retrieve information stored inside a relational database.

This is considered as the standard computer language for RDSs (i.e. Relational Database Systems). Modern database systems such as MySQL, Oracle, Informix, Sybase, and MS Access utilize SQL as their standard language.

The Main Advantages Offered by SQL

SQL allows you to do the following:

- Access information within relational database systems.

- Add descriptions for the information you'll store.

- Define and manipulate the data stored in your databases.

- Use other languages through its built-in libraries, pre-compilers, and modules.

- Generate and delete tables and databases.

- Generate, view, and store functions within your databases.

- Assign access rights on your tables and database objects.

How Does SQL Work?

Whenever you run SQL commands on a relational database management system, the system identifies the ideal way to process your request. Then, the SQL engine will interpret the activities involved.

The process outlined above involves different components. These are: Optimization Engines, Query Dispatcher, SQL Query Engine, and Classic Query Engine. The image below will show you the basic architecture of an SQL process:

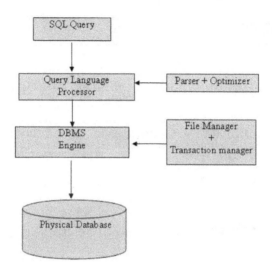

The Commands That You Can Use in SQL

This section of the book will explain the basic SQL commands. Study this material carefully since it can help you learn SQL within 2 weeks.

According to expert programmers, the standard commands in SQL are SELECT, CREATE, UPDATE, DROP, DELETE, and INSERT. Let's classify these commands according to their behavior:

The Data Definition Language (also known as DDL)

- CREATE – Generates a new object or table inside a database.

- ALTER – Edits existing objects within a database.

- DROP – Removes database objects.

The Data Manipulation Language (also known as DML)

- INSERT – Generates a new record in a database.

- UPDATE – Edits existing records in a database.

- DELETE – Removes existing database records.

The Data Control Language (also known as DCL)

- GRANT – Allows you to give access privileges to certain database users.

- REVOKE – Allows you to take back access privileges from certain users.

The Data Query Language (also known as DQL)

- SELECT – Allows you to retrieve records from your database.

Chapter 2 – The Basic Concepts of Relational Database Management Systems

SQL is a language you can use to interact with relational database management systems. Thus, you should also understand the basic characteristics of these database systems. This chapter will explain the basics of RDBMSs so that you can successfully learn SQL in 14 days.

What is a Database Table?

In a RDBMS, information is saved inside a database object known as a "table." A table is a set of related database entries and is composed of rows and columns.

You should know that tables are the most basic and common forms of information storage in relational database systems. Here's an example of a database table:

ID	Name	Sex	State
1	John	Male	New York
2	Mark	Male	Florida
3	Christian	Male	Texas
4	Paul	Male	Illinois
5	James	Male	Nevada
6	Peter	Male	Arkansas
7	Simon	Male	Virginia

Fields

Each database table contains smaller parts known as "fields." In the example given above, the fields are: ID, Sex, Name, and State.

Fields are columns inside a table that are created to retain certain information about each database record.

Rows

A row, also known as a "data record," is an individual database entry stored in a table. For instance, the table shown above has seven records. Here is a sample record:

1	John	Male	New York

Basically, records are horizontal entities found inside a table.

Columns

Columns are vertical entities found inside a table. They contain information related to a certain field. For instance, ID is one of the columns in the example given above. It represents the identification number of the listed people.

ID
1
2
3
4
5
6
7

Null Values

Null values in a database table are blank. That means fields that contain "NULL" are empty.

You should keep in mind that NULL values are different from zeroes and "spaces" (i.e. the character you'll get after hitting the spacebar). A field acquires NULL when the database user doesn't enter any value during table creation.

The Constraints in SQL

In SQL, a constraint is a rule applied on certain data columns. It is used to restrict the kind of information that can be stored in the table. Basically, constraints help you in ensuring the reliability and accuracy of your databases.

You can apply constraints on a tabular or columnar level. Thus, you may apply constraints on certain columns or entire tables.

Here are some of the popular constraints in the SQL programming language:

- UNIQUE – This constraint prevents data redundancy in your selected columns. For instance, you may need to prevent listed users from having the same identification number. Analyze the following example:

```
CREATE TABLE CUSTOMERS(
        ID    INT              NOT NULL,
        NAME VARCHAR (20)      NOT NULL,
        AGE   INT              NOT NULL UNIQUE,
        ADDRESS   CHAR (25) ,
        SALARY    DECIMAL (18, 2),
        PRIMARY KEY (ID)
);
```

This code creates a table named CUSTOMERS and divides it into five columns. The UNIQUE constraint is applied on the AGE column, so you can't enter two or more customers with identical age.

If you want to apply this constraint on an existing column, you may use the following syntax:

ALTER TABLE (insert name of table here)

MODIFY (insert name of column) (specify the value type) NOT NULL UNIQUE;

- DEFAULT – This constraint allows you to set default data. However, you can only use this if INSERT INTO (another SQL statement) doesn't have a particular value. Here's an example:

```
CREATE TABLE CUSTOMERS(
    ID    INT           NOT NULL,
    NAME VARCHAR (20)   NOT NULL,
    AGE  INT            NOT NULL,
    ADDRESS  CHAR (25) ,
    SALARY   DECIMAL (18, 2) DEFAULT 5000.00,
    PRIMARY KEY (ID)
);
```

This code generates a table named CUSTOMERS and divides it into 5 columns. As you can see, "5000.00" is tagged as the default value for the salary column. That means if you can't add any value using the INSERT INTO command, the column will receive 5000.00 automatically.

To remove this constraint, you may use the following syntax:

ALTER TABLE (insert name of table here)

ALTER COLUMN (insert name of column here) DROP DEFAULT;

- NOT NULL – Columns can contain NULL values. If you don't want to have NULL values in certain columns, however, you may utilize this constraint. This constraint will prevent the system from entering NULL values in the columns you specified.

Important Note: NULL values represent unknown information. Thus, they are different from "no information."

The screenshot below shows you how to apply the NOT NULL constraint using SQL:

```
CREATE TABLE CUSTOMERS(
    ID    INT            NOT NULL,
    NAME VARCHAR (20)    NOT NULL,
    AGE   INT            NOT NULL,
    ADDRESS  CHAR (25) ,
    SALARY   DECIMAL (18, 2),
    PRIMARY KEY (ID)
);
```

The code given above generates a table named CUSTOMERS and creates 5 columns. You cannot enter NULL values in ID, AGE, and NAME because the NOT NULL constraint is applied on them.

To apply NOT NULL on an existing column, use the following syntax:

ALTER TABLE (name of table here)

MODIFY (name of column) (specify value type) NOT NULL;

- CHECK – This constraint can check the values you are storing into the table. If the specified condition gives "false," you won't be able to add a value into your records. Analyze the code given below:

```
CREATE TABLE CUSTOMERS(
    ID    INT            NOT NULL,
    NAME VARCHAR (20)    NOT NULL,
    AGE   INT            NOT NULL CHECK (AGE >= 18),
    ADDRESS  CHAR (25) ,
    SALARY   DECIMAL (18, 2),
    PRIMARY KEY (ID)
);
```

That code creates a table named CUSTOMERS and divides it into five columns. The CHECK constraint is applied on AGE. Based on its condition (i.e. >= 18), you won't be able to add customers whose age is below 18.

To apply this constraint on an existing table, you should use the following syntax:

ALTER TABLE (name of table you want to edit)

MODIFY (name of column you want to use) (specify the value type) NOT NULL CHECK (name of column and the condition you want to apply);

- INDEX – You should use this constraint to generate or retrieve data quickly. When creating an index, you may select a single column or a set of columns. Active indices receive a ROWID for every row before they sort out the information.

  Good indices are necessary if you want to improve the reliability and performance of your databases. However, you should be extremely careful while creating an index. You should choose the fields that you'll use while running database searches. The SQL statement below creates a table named CUSTOMERS and divides it into 5 columns:

```
CREATE TABLE CUSTOMERS(
    ID      INT             NOT NULL,
    NAME VARCHAR (20)       NOT NULL,
    AGE   INT               NOT NULL,
    ADDRESS  CHAR (25) ,
    SALARY   DECIMAL (18, 2),
    PRIMARY KEY (ID)
);
```

- Primary Key – This is a field that identifies every record inside the table. When creating a primary key, you may use a single field or combine several ones. Keys that involve several fields are known as "composite keys." Primary keys must hold unique values (i.e. they won't accept duplicate or NULL values).

- How to assign a primary key while creating a new table - Use the following syntax when defining a primary key in your new tables:

```
CREATE TABLE CUSTOMERS(
    ID    INT           NOT NULL,
    NAME VARCHAR (20)   NOT NULL,
    AGE  INT            NOT NULL,
    ADDRESS  CHAR (25) ,
    SALARY   DECIMAL (18, 2),
    PRIMARY KEY (ID)
);
```

- How to assign a primary key for an existing table – Here's the syntax you should use:

ALTER TABLE (insert name of table here) ADD PRIMARY KEY (specify the name of column here);

Important Note: If you'll assign a column as the primary key, you have to make sure that it won't accept NULL values.

- How to delete a primary key - To disable a primary key, you should use the following syntax:

ALTER TABLE (name of table) DROP PRIMARY KEY;

- Foreign Key – This key allows you to link data tables. For this reason, some programmers refer to foreign keys as "referencing keys."

Foreign keys are columns whose values are identical to the primary key of another table. That means the primary key of one table must match the foreign key of a different table.

To help you understand this concept, let's use two sample tables: CUSTOMERS and ORDERS.

The CUSTOMERS table:

```
CREATE TABLE CUSTOMERS(
      ID    INT              NOT NULL,
      NAME VARCHAR (20)      NOT NULL,
      AGE   INT              NOT NULL,
      ADDRESS  CHAR (25) ,
      SALARY   DECIMAL (18, 2),
      PRIMARY KEY (ID)
);
```

The ORDERS table:

```
CREATE TABLE ORDERS (
      ID         INT        NOT NULL,
      DATE       DATETIME,
      CUSTOMER_ID INT references CUSTOMERS(ID),
      AMOUNT   double,
      PRIMARY KEY (ID)
);
```

If you want to assign a foreign key on an existing table, you should use the following syntax:

ALTER TABLE (insert the table's name here)

ADD FOREIGN KEY (specify the column you want to use as the foreign key) REFERENCES (name of the table you want to use as a reference) (name of the second table's primary key);

Chapter 3: The Syntax of SQL Statements

The SQL language uses a distinct collection of rules known as "syntax." This chapter will teach you the basic syntax used in SQL. Study this material carefully since it will help you master this computer language in just 2 weeks.

Each SQL command begins with one of the following keywords: USE, DROP, SHOW, ALTER, UPDATE, INSERT, SELECT, DELETE, or CREATE. Additionally, each command ends with a semicolon.

You should know that SQL statements are not case sensitive. That means DELETE and delete are identical when it comes to SQL commands. If you are using MySQL, however, you should enter names as they appear on the database.

The Syntax of Basic SQL Commands

The SELECT Statement

```
SELECT column1, column2....columnN
FROM    table_name;
```

This statement has the following clauses:

- The DISTINCT Clause -

```
SELECT DISTINCT column1, column2....columnN
FROM    table_name;
```

- The WHERE Clause -

```
SELECT column1, column2....columnN
FROM    table name
WHERE   CONDITION;
```

- The AND/OR Clause -

```
SELECT column1, column2....columnN
FROM    table name
WHERE   CONDITION-1 {AND|OR} CONDITION-2;
```

- The IN Clause –

```
SELECT column1, column2....columnN
FROM    table name
WHERE   column_name IN (val-1, val-2,...val-N);
```

- The BETWEEN Clause –

```
SELECT column1, column2....columnN
FROM    table_name
WHERE   column_name BETWEEN val-1 AND val-2;
```

- The LIKE Clause –

```
SELECT column1, column2....columnN
FROM    table name
WHERE   column_name LIKE { PATTERN };
```

- The ORDER BY Clause –

```
SELECT column1, column2....columnN
FROM    table name
WHERE   CONDITION
ORDER BY column_name {ASC|DESC};
```

- The GROUP BY Clause –

```
SELECT SUM(column name)
FROM    table name
WHERE   CONDITION
GROUP BY column_name;
```

- The COUNT Clause –

```
SELECT COUNT(column name)
FROM    table name
WHERE   CONDITION;
```

- The HAVING Clause –

```
SELECT SUM(column name)
FROM    table name
WHERE   CONDITION
GROUP BY column name
HAVING (arithematic function condition);
```

The CREATE TABLE Command

```
CREATE TABLE table_name(
column1 datatype,
column2 datatype,
column3 datatype,
.....
columnN datatype,
PRIMARY KEY( one or more columns )
);
```

The DROP TABLE Command

```
DROP TABLE table_name;
```

The CREATE INDEX Command

```
CREATE UNIQUE INDEX index name
ON table_name ( column1, column2,...columnN);
```

The DROP INDEX Command

```
ALTER TABLE table name
DROP INDEX index_name;
```

The DESC Command

```
DESC table_name;
```

The TRUNCATE TABLE Command

```
TRUNCATE TABLE table_name;
```

The ALTER TABLE Command

```
ALTER TABLE table_name {ADD|DROP|MODIFY} column_name {data_ype};
```

The ALTER TABLE Command (for renaming tables)

```
ALTER TABLE table_name RENAME TO new_table_name;
```

The INSERT INTO Command

```
INSERT INTO table_name( column1, column2....columnN)
VALUES ( value1, value2....valueN);
```

The UPDATE Command

```
UPDATE table_name
SET column1 = value1, column2 = value2....columnN=valueN
[ WHERE  CONDITION ];
```

The DELETE Command

```
DELETE FROM table name
WHERE   {CONDITION};
```

The CREATE DATABASE Command

```
CREATE DATABASE database_name;
```

The DROP Database Command

```
DROP DATABASE database_name;
```

The USE Command

```
USE DATABASE database_name;
```

The COMMIT Command

```
COMMIT;
```

The ROLLBACK Command

```
ROLLBACK;
```

Chapter 4: The Different Data Types in SQL

In the SQL language, data type is a characteristic that determines the type of any database object. All columns, variables, and expressions involve data types in SQL.

You should indicate data types while generating new tables. Additionally, you have to select data types for your tables based on your needs.

This computer language supports many types of data. Let's divide these types into six major categories:

1. *Exact Numeric*

DATA TYPE	FROM	TO
Bigint	-9,223,372,036,854,775,808	9,223,372,036,854,775,807
Int	-2,147,483,648	2,147,483,647
Smallint	-32,768	32,767
Tinyint	0	255
Bit	0	1
Decimal	-10^38 +1	10^38 -1
Numeric	-10^38 +1	10^38 -1
Money	-922,337,203,685,477.5808	+922,337,203,685,477.5807
Smallmoney	-214,748.3648	+214,748.3647

2. *Approximate Numeric*

DATA TYPE	FROM	TO
Float	-1.79E + 308	1.79E + 308
Real	-3.40E + 38	3.40E + 38

3. Time and Date

DATA TYPE	FROM	TO
Datetime	Jan 1, 1753	Dec 31, 9999
Smalldatetime	Jan 1, 1900	Jun 6, 2079
Date	Stores a date like June 30, 1991	
Time	Stores a time of day like 12:30 P.M.	

4. *Character Strings* – This is divided into two subcategories:

a. *Unicode Strings*

DATA TYPE	Description
Nchar	Maximum length of 4,000 characters.(Fixed length Unicode)
Nvarchar	Maximum length of 4,000 characters.(Variable length Unicode)
nvarchar(max)	Maximum length of 231characters (SQL Server 2005 only).(Variable length Unicode)
Ntext	Maximum length of 1,073,741,823 characters. (Variable length Unicode)

b. *Non-Unicode Strings*

DATA TYPE	FROM	TO
Char	Char	Maximum length of 8,000 characters.(Fixed length non-Unicode characters)
Varchar	Varchar	Maximum of 8,000 characters.(Variable-length non-Unicode data).
varchar(max)	varchar(max)	Maximum length of 231characters, Variable-length non-Unicode data (SQL Server 2005 only).
Text	text	Variable-length non-Unicode data with a maximum length of 2,147,483,647 characters.

5. *Binary*

DATA TYPE	Description
Binary	Maximum length of 8,000 bytes(Fixed-length binary data)
Varbinary	Maximum length of 8,000 bytes.(Variable length binary data)
varbinary(max)	Maximum length of 231 bytes (SQL Server 2005 only). (Variable length Binary data)
Image	Maximum length of 2,147,483,647 bytes. (Variable length Binary Data)

6. *Miscellaneous*

This category involves the following data types:

- timestamp – This data type stores a unique number that becomes updated whenever a row becomes updated. You may access this unique number in any part of your database.

- xml – This data type stores XML (i.e. Extensible Markup Language) information. You may save XML data in columns or variables.

- table – This type saves the results of your database queries so that you can use them in the future.

- cursor – This data type allows you to make references to any cursor object in your database.

- sql_variant – This can store the values of all SQL-compatible data types, except timestamp, text, and next.

- unique identifier – This data type can store GUIDs (i.e. Globally Unique Identifiers).

Chapter 5: The Operators in the SQL Language

Operators are reserved words or characters that you can use for your SQL commands. Generally, operators are used in the WHERE section of your commands to conduct operations (e.g. comparisons, mathematical operations, etc.).

You can use an operator to specify a condition in your SQL statements. In some cases, you may utilize an operator as a conjunction if your commands involve multiple conditions.

This chapter will discuss the four types of operators supported by SQL:

- Logical Operators
- Arithmetic Operators
- Comparison Operators
- Operators that can nullify conditions

The Logical Operators

These are the logical operators that you can use in the SQL computer language:

- IN – You can use this operator to compare a value against your specified literal values.

- OR – This operator combines various conditions in the WHERE section of your SQL commands.

- AND – This operator allows you to include multiple conditions in the WHERE clause of your SQL commands.

- ALL – This operator compares a value against values that are inside a different value set.

- ANY – This operator uses a condition to perform comparisons.

- LIKE – This operator uses wildcard operators to compare values against similar ones.

- UNIQUE – This operator checks the uniqueness of your entries. To accomplish this, the UNIQUE operator scans the entire table and searches for redundant data.

- EXISTS – This operator searches for rows that meet specified criteria.

- BETWEEN – This operator searches for values that are inside a certain range. When using BETWEEN, you should indicate the highest value and the lowest value.

- IS NULL – This operator compares a value against a NULL value.

The Arithmetic Operators

To help you understand these operators, let's use two sample variables: x = 1; y = 2.

- "+" – You should use this operator to perform addition. For instance, x + y = 3.

- "-" – You must use this operator to perform subtraction. It will subtract the value of the right operand from that of the left operand. For example, y − x = 1.

- "*" – You should use this operator when performing multiplication. Here's an example: x * y = 2.

- "/" – You should use this operator when performing division. For example: y / x = 2.

The Comparison Operators

Let's assume that x = 2 and y = 4.

- "=" – This operator checks the equality of two values. If the values are equal, the condition is true. For example: (x = y) is not true.

- "!=" – This operator checks the equality of two values. If the values are unequal, the condition is true. For example: (y != x) is true.

- "<>" – This operator is the same as "!=". For example: (x <> y) is true.

- ">" – This operator checks if the left operand's value is greater than that of the right operand. If it is, the condition is true. For instance: (y > x) is true.

- "<" – This operator checks whether the left operand's value is less than that of the right operand. If it is, the condition is true. For instance: (x < y) is true.

- ">=" – This operator checks if the left operand's value is greater than or equal to that of the right operand. If it is, the condition is true. For example: (y >= x) is true.

- "<=" – This operator checks if the left operand's value is lesser than or equal to that of the right operand. If it is, the condition is true. For instance: (x <= y) is true.

The Operator that can Nullify Conditions

- NOT – This operator can reverse the function of the logical operator you'll use it with. For example: NOT IN, NOT EXISTS, NOT BETWEEN, etc.

Chapter 6: The SQL Expressions

Basically, an expression is a group of values, functions, and operators. SQL expressions can help you evaluate database values.

In this computer language, an expression is a formula that you must write using a query language. You may also use an expression to run a database query for certain pieces of information.

The Syntax

Here is the format of the SELECT command:

```
SELECT column1, column2, columnN
FROM table name
WHERE [CONDITION|EXPRESSION];
```

Now, let's talk about the expressions supported by SQL:

The Boolean Expressions – These expressions retrieve data by matching a single value. Here is the basic syntax of a Boolean expression:

```
SELECT column1, column2, columnN
FROM table name
WHERE SINGLE VALUE MATCHTING EXPRESSION;
```

The Numeric Expressions – You can use these expressions to conduct mathematical operations in your database queries. Here is the syntax that you should use:

```
SELECT numerical expression as  OPERATION NAME
[FROM table_name
WHERE CONDITION] ;
```

The Date Expressions – These expressions give you the time and date information of your system.

Chapter 7: How to Use SQL in Your Databases

This chapter will teach you how to apply SQL commands on your own databases. By reading this material, you'll be able to interact with relational databases using the SQL computer language. This material is extremely important because it will help you master the basics of SQL in just 2 weeks.

How to Create a Database

To create a new database, you should use the CREATE DATABASE command. Here's the syntax that you should follow:

```
CREATE DATABASE DatabaseName;
```

Important Note: Relational database management systems require unique database names.

Let's use the CREATE DATABASE command to generate a new database.

CREATE DATABASE sample;

The command given above creates a new database named "sample."

Important Note: You won't be able to create a new database if you don't have admin privileges.

How to Delete a Database

In the SQL language, you use the DROP DATABASE command to delete an active database. Use the following syntax:

DROP DATABASE (insert the name of your database);

For example, let's say you want to delete a database named "sample." Here's the SQL command you need to use:

DROP DATABASE sample;

Important Note: You should be extremely careful when using this command. Keep in mind that deleting a database involves permanent loss of data.

How to Select a Database

If you own multiple databases, you have to make sure that you are performing your desired operations on the right database/s. You should utilize the USE command to choose an existing database. Analyze the following syntax:

USE (insert name of the database here)

For instance, to select a database named "sample," use the following SQL command:

USE sample

How to Create a Table

If you are creating a new table, you should name that table and define its columns and supported data types. You should use the CREATE TABLE command to accomplish this task. Here's the syntax you should follow:

```
CREATE TABLE table name(
    column1 datatype,
    column2 datatype,
    column3 datatype,
    . . . . .
    columnN datatype,
    PRIMARY KEY( one or more columns )
);
```

Basically, "CREATE TABLE" is a keyword that informs the system about your desire to create a new table. The identifier or name of your table comes after the CREATE TABLE command.

Then, create a list that defines the columns and data types that you want to use. Don't worry if this is a bit confusing. You'll understand this once you have analyzed the example given below.

How to Create a New Table from an Existing One

You may copy an existing table by combining two commands: SELECT and CREATE TABLE.

By default, the table that you'll get will have the column definitions of the old one. However, you may select certain columns from the old table and discard the others. That means you may modify the new table according to your needs.

If you'll succeed in using this command, the new table will acquire the current values of the old table. Here's the syntax that you should use:

```
CREATE TABLE NEW_TABLE_NAME AS
    SELECT [ column1, column2...columnN ]
    FROM EXISTING TABLE NAME
    [ WHERE ]
```

For instance, you would like to use a table named EMPLOYEES to generate a new one (let's say you'd like to call it "COMPENSATION"). Then, you want to copy two of the columns inside the EMPLOYEES table: NAME and SALARY. To accomplish this task, you can use the following SQL code:

CREATE TABLE COMPENSATION AS

    SELECT NAME, SALARY

    FROM EMPLOYEES;

The code given above creates a new table named COMPENSATION, which has two columns: NAME and SALARY. Additionally, these columns will acquire the values found in the old table (i.e. EMPLOYEES).

How to Delete a Table

You can use the DROP TABLE command to delete a table and all the information it contains (e.g. data, constraints, indexes, etc.).

Important Note: You have to be careful when using this command. Remember that it involves the permanent removal of stored information. If you'll drop the wrong table, you will face serious problems regarding your database.

The syntax of this command is:

DROP TABLE (insert the table's name here);

For example: *DROP TABLE sample*

The command given above deletes a table named "sample" from your database.

How to Add New Data Rows

The INSERT INTO command allows you to add new data rows to an existing table. This command involves two syntaxes:

The First Syntax

```
INSERT INTO TABLE NAME (column1, column2, column3,...columnN)]
VALUES (value1, value2, value3,...valueN);
```

You should use this syntax if you want to add data into certain columns.

The Second Syntax

```
INSERT INTO TABLE_NAME VALUES (value1,value2,value3,...valueN);
```

You must use this syntax if you want to add values to all of the columns of your table. That means you won't have to identify the columns you are working on. However, make sure that the sequence of the values is the same as that of the existing columns in the table.

How to Retrieve Data from a Table

You may use the SELECT command to retrieve data from a table. Here, SQL will present the search results as a new table. These new tables are known as "result sets."

The syntax of the SELECT command is:

```
SELECT column1, column2, columnN FROM table_name;
```

In this syntax, column1, column2, etc., are the fields that you like to retrieve. If you like to retrieve all of the fields inside a table, you may use this syntax:

```
SELECT * FROM table_name;
```

The WHERE Clause

WHERE is an SQL clause that specifies a condition while retrieving information from your chosen table/s.

If your specified condition is met, this clause will retrieve specific values from your table. In general, you should use WHERE to filter and retrieve the records that you need.

You may also use WHERE in other SQL commands such as DELETE and UPDATE. You'll learn about these commands later on.

The syntax that you should use is:

```
SELECT column1, column2, columnN
FROM table name
WHERE [condition]
```

You may use logical or comparison operators to set a condition for your WHERE clause.

How to Combine Various Conditions

SQL allows you to combine different conditions on your database queries. You just have to include the OR and AND operators in your SQL commands. SQL users refer to OR and AND as conjunctive operators.

Basically, the conjunctive operators allow you to perform multiple comparisons in a single SQL command. Let's discuss OR first:

OR

You may use this operator to combine various conditions in a command's WHERE clause. The syntax of this operator is:

```
SELECT column1, column2, columnN
FROM table name
WHERE [condition1] OR [condition2]...OR [conditionN]
```

N represents the quantity of conditions that you can combine using OR. Your SQL statements will perform an action only if one of your specified conditions is true.

AND

This operator allows you to place several conditions in the WHERE clause of an SQL command. Here's the syntax that you should use:

```
SELECT column1, column2, columnN
FROM table name
WHERE [condition1] AND [condition2]...AND [conditionN];
```

"N" represents the quantity of conditions that you can combine. Keep in mind that your SQL command will only perform an action if all of the conditions are true.

How to Modify Existing Records

In the SQL language, you may edit existing records using the UPDATE query. This query, which is applied on the WHERE clause, allows you to edit data rows. Here's the syntax that you should use:

```
UPDATE table name
SET column1 = value1, column2 = value2...., columnN = valueN
WHERE [condition];
```

How to Delete Records

If you want to delete records, you may use SQL's DELETE Query. You can combine this query with SELECT to delete certain rows. On the other hand, you may use DELETE as a standalone query to delete all of the data rows. Here's the syntax of this query:

DELETE FROM the_table's_name

WHERE [specify you condition/s];

If you need to remove all the records from a table, you may simply remove the WHERE clause. Thus, the syntax will be:

DELETE FROM the_table's_name;

How to Perform Comparisons Through Wildcard Operators

In SQL, you may use wildcard operators to compare a value against similar values. You just have to include these operators in the LIKE clause of your SQL commands. Here are the wildcard operators that you can use with LIKE:

- The underscore (i.e. "_")
- The percent symbol (i.e. "%")

You should use an underscore if you want to represent a single character or number. You must use the percent sign, on the other hand, if you want to represent, 0, 1, or several characters. You may combine these wildcard operators in your SQL statements.

Here is the syntax of the wildcard operators:

```
SELECT FROM table name
WHERE column LIKE 'XXXX%'

or

SELECT FROM table name
WHERE column LIKE '%XXXX%'

or

SELECT FROM table name
WHERE column LIKE 'XXXX '

or

SELECT FROM table name
WHERE column LIKE ' XXXX'

or

SELECT FROM table_name
WHERE column LIKE '_XXXX_'
```

How to Use the TOP Clause

The TOP clause allows you to retrieve a number or percentage from your data tables.

Important Note: Some databases are not compatible with this clause. For instance, MySQL uses LIMIT to retrieve records.

The syntax of a SELECT command with the TOP clause is:

```
SELECT TOP number|percent column name(s)
FROM table name
WHERE [condition]
```

How to Sort Data

SQL offers ORDER BY, a clause that sorts data in descending or ascending order, depending on the column/s you use as a basis. The syntax that you should is:

```
SELECT column-list
FROM table name
[WHERE condition]
[ORDER BY column1, column2, .. columnN] [ASC | DESC];
```

You may include multiple columns in this clause. However, make sure that all of the columns you want to use are inside the column-list.

How to Mix the Results of Multiple SELECT Commands

In SQL, you may combine results from multiple SELECT commands while preventing redundant rows. You just have to use the UNION clause.

To use this clause, your SELECT statements should have the same quantity of selected columns and column expressions. The statements must also have the same type of data and column arrangement. However, the statements don't need to have identical lengths.

The syntax for this clause is:

```
SELECT column1 [, column2 ]
FROM table1 [, table2 ]
[WHERE condition]

UNION

SELECT column1 [, column2 ]
FROM table1 [, table2 ]
[WHERE condition]
```

Chapter 8: How to Combine Records Using SQL

You may use the JOIN clause to combine records from multiple databases. Basically, JOIN is a method that can combine fields from different tables.

The Different Types of JOIN

The SQL computer language supports different kinds of JOIN. These are:

- SELF JOIN – You can use this if you want to link a table to itself as if you are working on different tables. While doing this, you should rename at least one table in your SQL command.

- RIGHT JOIN – This JOIN retrieves all data rows from the right table. SQL will complete this task even if no matches exist between the two tables.

- LEFT JOIN – This JOIN returns all data rows from the left table. The SQL language will complete this even if no matches exist between the tables involved.

- FULL JOIN – This JOIN retrieves data rows if one of the tables has a match.

- INNER JOIN – This returns data rows if both tables have a match.

- CARTESIAN JOIN – This JOIN retrieves the Cartesian values of the record sets from the joined tables.

Let's discuss each JOIN in detail:

The INNER JOIN

This is one of the most important joins in SQL. It generates a new table by mixing the column values of different tables. The database query checks the rows of all tables to determine if there are row pairs that meet the join-predicate's requirements. If the pairs of rows satisfy the join-predicate, the values for those rows are placed in a new table. Here's the syntax that you should use:

```
SELECT table1.column1, table2.column2...
FROM table1
INNER JOIN table2
ON table1.common_filed = table2.common_field;
```

The LEFT JOIN

This JOIN retrieves all data rows from the left table. SQL does this even if the right table doesn't have any match. Thus, if your command's ON clause has o matches with the right table, you'll still get a data row from the process. However, the columns from the right table will have NULL values inside them.

The syntax of this join is:

```
SELECT table1.column1, table2.column2...
FROM table1
LEFT JOIN table2
ON table1.common_filed = table2.common_field;
```

The RIGHT JOIN

This JOIN returns all data rows from the table on the right. The SQL language will do this even if the left table doesn't have any match. Basically, you'll still get at least one data row from this process even if your command's ON clause has no matches with the left table. However, the columns from the left table will contain NULL values.

The syntax of this join is:

```
SELECT table1.column1, table2.column2...
FROM table1
RIGHT JOIN table2
ON table1.common_filed = table2.common_field;
```

The FULL JOIN

This SQL JOIN mixes the results of the left and right joins. The new table will have all of the records from the two tables. Here's the syntax that you should use:

```
SELECT table1.column1, table2.column2...
FROM table1
FULL JOIN table2
ON table1.common_filed = table2.common_field;
```

Important Note: FULL JOIN uses NULL values to fill records that don't match.

The SELF JOIN

You should use this join if you want to link a table to itself. As noted earlier, you have to rename at least one of the tables in your SQL statement.

The syntax of this JOIN is:

```
SELECT a.column name, b.column name...
FROM table1 a, table1 b
WHERE a.common_filed = b.common_field;
```

The CARTESIAN JOIN

This JOIN retrieves the Cartesian products of the record sets from the tables that you are using. Because of this, SQL users consider this as an INNER JOIN whose join-condition is always true. The syntax of the CARTESIAN JOIN is:

```
SELECT table1.column1, table2.column2...
FROM  table1, table2 [, table3 ]
```

Conclusion

Thank you again for downloading this book!

I hope this book was able to help you learn the basics of SQL in just two weeks.

The next step is to use this computer language in creating and managing your own databases.

Finally, if you enjoyed this book, then I'd like to ask you for a favor, would you be kind enough to leave a review for this book on Amazon? It'd be greatly appreciated!

Please leave a review on Amazon!

Thank you and good luck!